THE "WOMEN OF RENOWN" SERIES

ELIZABETH
GARRETT ANDERSON

BY

H. BELLIS, L.L.A.

British Library Cataloguing-in-Publication Data
A catalogue record for this book is available from the
British Library

CONTENTS

Elizabeth Garrett Anderson

Elizabeth Garrett Anderson was born on 9 June 1836, in London, England. She was the second of the eleven children of Newson Garrett and his wife Louisa née Dunnell. She became famous as a physician and feminist, being the first British woman to qualify as a physician and surgeon.

The Garrett family lived in a pleasant Georgian house in Aldeburgh, Suffolk, until 1852, and thereafter in Alde House; a mansion on a hill behind the town. Newson Garrett was a prosperous businessman, who owned a barley and coal merchants. Due to the thriving industrial revolution then taking place, Garrett grew up in an atmosphere of 'triumphant economic pioneering', and as a result of this, she was as much at home among the upper classes as she was amongst the fishing folk of the area. This was to be one of Garrett's greatest boons in later life.

Elizabeth was educated at home until the age of thirteen, thereafter attending the *Boarding School for Ladies* in Blackheath, London. And whilst Garrett later recalled her distain for the 'stupidity of her teachers', it was during these school days that she established a love of reading; Tennyson, Wordsworth, Milton, Coleridge, Thackeray and Eliot were among her favourites. In 1859, Garrett joined the *Society for Promoting the Employment of Women,* and it was here that she was introduced to Dr. Elizabeth Blackwell; the first female to become a doctor in the USA (1849). This meeting prompted Garrett to embark on her medical career. After several unsuccessful visits to leading doctors in Harley Street, Garrett decided to spend six months as a hospital nurse at Middlesex Hospital, London in 1860. Eventually she was allowed into the dissecting room and the chemistry lectures. Over time, the male students resented her presence however, and petitioned against her re-admittance as a fellow student in 1861. They were successful, but during the following four years, Garrett continued her battle to qualify by studying privately with various professors, including some at the *University of St Andrews, Edinburgh Royal Maternity* and the *London Hospital Medical School.* In 1864 she finally obtained a licence to practice medicine from the *Society of Apothecaries.* Due to being prevented from working in any existing medical establishments, Garrett opened her own practice in late 1865. It was scarcely attended at first, but when the cholera epidemic broke out in 1866, many Londoners forgot their prejudices against a woman physician. Garrett also opened the *St. Mary's Dispensary for Women and Children* (largely catering for poorer women), in which she tended to 3000 new patients in the first year alone. In 1870, she became the first woman in Britain to be appointed to an official medical post; as a visiting physician to the *East London Hospital for*

Children, a position which she held for the next three years.

Garrett married in 1871, to James George Skelton Anderson, but to her credit, did not give up any of her professional practice. She enjoyed a happy married life, and had three children; Louisa, Margaret (who unfortunately died at the age of one from meningitis) and Alan. In 1874, alongside caring for her own young children, Garrett founded the *London School of Medicine*; the only teaching hospital in Britain to offer courses for women. She worked there for the rest of her career and served as Dean of the school from 1883 to 1902. Perhaps unsurprisingly, Garrett was heavily involved in the suffrage movement, especially after her husband's death from a stroke in 1907. On 9 November 1908, she was elected mayor of Aldeburgh, the first female mayor in England, and as part of this role, gave many speeches in support of women's suffrage. The increasing militancy of the movement led to her withdrawal soon afterwards though. She died on 17th December 1917, at the age of eighty-one, and is buried in Aldeburgh.

ELIZABETH GARRETT ANDERSON

ELIZABETH
GARRETT ANDERSON

THE guard blew his horn!

The driver cracked his whip!

The hooves of the horses struck sparks from the newly-macadamed road, and the coach rolled merrily on its way.

Louisa and Elizabeth, from their seat beside the driver, turned to wave a last farewell to their father, Mr. Garrett, who stood by the pony trap, now half hidden in a cloud of dust. And what a half-tearful, half-joyful farewell it was!

ADVENTUROUS JOURNEY

The two girls were sad to be leaving their happy home in Aldeburgh, but they were off to their first school. Naturally they were eager and excited as they set out on this new adventure.

And a real adventure it was, in those days, just over a hundred years ago.

First there was the journey itself.

There were, at that time, a few of those new and rather alarming railroads in England.

Along these railroads, iron monsters, driven by steam, snorted and clanged their noisy way at the terrific rate of thirty miles an hour. But the railway had not yet reached Aldeburgh.

Indeed, even the Stage Coaches did not call at the sleepy little place, for the main road was four miles away.

When, a few years earlier, the Garrett family had removed from London to this little fishing village they had come by water. The two eldest girls, Louisa and Elizabeth, still remembered the discomforts of the journey and the difficulties of landing young children and furniture from open boats.

Now they were going back to London by road and rail! What a thrilling experience!

Father had brought them and their luggage in the pony trap from their home, to the main road where they had joined the coach.

This, drawn by its four splendid horses, was now bowling along the turnpike road to Ipswich between hedges white with dust.

At Ipswich the two girls, aged fifteen and thirteen, were met by a friend of the family, and seen safely aboard the steam-drawn train which took them swiftly to London.

Here they were met by an uncle, who escorted them to a four-wheeled "growler" with straw on the floor!

The growler, or cab, was drawn by a wretchedly thin old horse, so the girls had plenty of time to see something of the streets of London as they wound their way slowly from the station to Blackheath.

What a thrilling journey they had had—pony trap, stage coach, steam train and growler! And what a long time they had been on the way, though only forty miles or so separated Blackheath from their home at Aldeburgh.

But their minds were already leaping forward to the second stage of their adventure.

Ah! Here at last was their school! What sort of a place

would it be? How anxiously the girls, who had seldom been away from home, leaned forward to catch the first glimpse of their new abode!

WORTHY ESTABLISHMENT

There were very few schools for girls in 1849, and Mr. Garrett had taken great pains to find what he considered a suitable one for his growing daughters.

He had finally decided on the *Academy for the Daughters of Gentlemen* at Blackheath.

This school was kept by Miss Browning and her sister, aunts of Robert Browning, who was just then making a name for himself as a poet.

Louisa and Elizabeth were full of wonder as to what life in this establishment would be like.

The girls were met on their arrival by Miss Browning herself, and all their lives they retained a vivid memory of this kindly and forceful woman.

She was a very large person, and delighted in dressing herself in brightly-coloured clothes, decorated with numerous ribbons and bows. She did not mind mixing her colours, and a dress of vivid orange and green might be decked with ribbons of purple and red.

She had many other little oddities which amused the girls, but she had a striking personality and sent many of her pupils away with a thirst for knowledge, which they retained all their lives.

Mr. Garrett had agreed to pay for all the "extras" which the school provided. Among other things, he had stipulated that the girls were to have a hot bath once a week.

Very few houses, even large mansions, possessed bathrooms a hundred years ago. Windsor Castle had only just had one installed, so no wonder the girls' weekly bath was regarded as something rather odd.

Each Saturday evening a tub, used for laundry work, was placed in front of the kitchen fire and surrounded by jugs of hot water. Here, screened by a huge towel-horse, the girls in turn took their bath, much to the amusement of other pupils, who called them "the bathing Garretts."

Louisa and Elizabeth remained at this school for two years. They left it with regret, and a keen determination to continue their studies at home.

AN EXCITING SUMMER

In the summer of 1851 their Uncle Richard escorted the girls to the Great Exhibition which had been organized by the Prince Consort. This was held in the huge glass house afterwards known as the Crystal Palace.

The visit was keenly enjoyed by the two eager young people, who flitted here and there in their crinolines and poke bonnets. Each wore a dainty shawl over her flowery dress, and each carried a tiny parasol in a mittened hand, for the sun must not be allowed to spoil a young girl's delicate complexion.

After a short visit to the Continent Louisa and Elizabeth returned to Aldeburgh, where Mr. Garrett had now a large mansion surrounded by gardens, paddocks, glass-houses, kitchen gardens and piggeries.

He added a laundry, and even an ice-house. Since Turkish baths were just becoming fashionable, nothing would satisfy him but that he should build one of these in his grounds. It was called by his old servants "Master's Sweatin' House."

Life in high, rambling Alde House was a very happy affair.

There were now six girls and three boys in the family and

a constant coming and going of cousins and friends. In the summer the country and the sea provided plenty of scope for amusement. In the winter there were frequent dances and parties in their own home or at the homes of friends.

Often these meant a journey in an old farm cart, its bottom covered with straw. But what of that? It was all part of the fun!

There were also visits to London, and even to far-distant Gateshead.

EAGER CROWDS HURRY TO THE GREAT EXHIBITION

Here lived Jane and Annie Crowe with whom the Garrett girls had become very friendly during their stay at the Blackheath School.

On the first of these visits they met Emily Davies, the daughter of the Rector of Gateshead.

This quiet young lady was six years older than Elizabeth, but she was to have a great influence on her future life, and indeed on the lives of thousands of other girls who came after her.

In 1857 Louisa married James Smith and went to live in London.

Elizabeth, who was now twenty-one years of age, took her place as the eldest daughter of the house. She went visiting with her mother and helped the younger children with their lessons. She tried to keep up her own studies and wrote numerous letters, particularly to Emily Davies.

She was not unhappy at home, and yet, as time went on, she began to feel that life should hold something more, for women of intelligence, than the aimless existence to which most of them were condemned.

She realized that she was very fortunate in her home. Everything was provided for her, and probably always would be, yet she was never made to feel inferior to her brothers, as many girls were at that time.

GRADUAL AWAKENING

But she knew that the majority of women in this and in most other countries were not so lucky.

Since the introduction of machinery and the Industrial Revolution many women of the poorer classes had been forced to go out to work, and Elizabeth knew from her reading and from her correspondence with Emily Davies that they often worked under terrible conditions for a very low wage.

On the other hand, there was practically no work available for girls whose parents were not quite so poor. If, as so often happened, a young woman found herself practically penniless on the death of her father, there was nothing she could do but take a post as a poorly-paid governess.

She had no training of any sort. True, Florence Nightingale was at this time struggling to make nursing a worthwhile profession for women, but as yet her battle had not been won.

Even worse than all this, in the eyes of a few women who were feeling a growing need for independence, was the fact that the law of the country did not allow a woman any rights at all. She apparently existed only by the courtesy of men.

If her father or any other relative left her any money this became, when she married, the property of her husband, and she must ask him for every penny she required.

From a painting in the possession of the Royal Free Hospital,
London

ELIZABETH GARRETT ANDERSON

If she lost her purse when out shopping it was described as "the property of her husband."

She had no vote, no voice in the government of her town or country. And, of course, she had no chance of making a career for herself in any of the professions.

Thoughtful women all over the land were beginning to feel that this was all wrong. Why should so many doors be fast barred against a person of intelligence just because she was a woman?

There were very few schools which provided higher education for girls. Even if they could prove that they had the brains and ability equal to that of most men, they could not go to a university.

They could not become doctors, lawyers, ministers of the gospel, clerks or secretaries.

Even the business of dressing a lady's hair was supposed to be beyond a woman. "Why, madam, it took even me a fortnight to learn the business," replied one indignant hairdresser when one of his customers asked if her daughter could take up hairdressing as a career.

Many women were beginning to wonder if it was right for them to be always treated as the inferiors of men. But while many wondered and repined, a few bold spirits began to put up some resistance. They determined to sweep away some of the unjust restrictions which hemmed in women on every hand.

One of these women was Emily Davies, the quiet, little, unassuming daughter of a Gateshead rector.

As she went about her father's parish she came to realize more and more how aimless and empty were the lives of women who were comfortably housed: how sordid and cruel the lives of the very poor.

"But how can people who have not learnt to *do* anything find anything to do?" she asked herself. "Women must learn. They must be taught. They have great powers within themselves. They must be trained as their brothers are trained, and so they will become free to use their powers in public service."

She discussed these ideas with Elizabeth Garrett when they met in Gateshead, and by correspondence when they were apart, and Elizabeth found them stimulating and thought-provoking.

What could she do in her comfortable home to free herself and others like her from the bonds which prevented them from living a full, satisfying and useful life?

In 1859, when she was about twenty-three years old, Elizabeth was again invited to Gateshead.

On her way north she spent a few days with her sister

Louisa in London, and there she met another eager pioneer, Dr. Elizabeth Blackwell.

FIRST WOMAN DOCTOR

Elizabeth Blackwell was born in Bristol, but when she was about eleven years old her family emigrated to America.

On the death of her father she had to earn her living and help with the younger children, so she began to teach.

She was a very intelligent girl, and one day a friend asked her why she did not study medicine. "If I could only have been treated by a lady doctor, my worst sufferings would have been spared," said this friend.

The idea appealed to Miss Blackwell, but it was necessary for her to earn money. So she went on teaching by day and spent long hours in the evenings studying medical books.

After a few years she applied for admission to the medical colleges. No less than sixteen of these refused her, on the grounds that she was a woman. But she persevered, and at last one college near New York agreed to accept her.

In 1849 she received her diploma, and became the first qualified woman doctor.

In 1858 she came to England and gave three lectures on "Medicine as a Profession for Ladies."

Elizabeth Garrett attended these lectures and when

she reached Gateshead she had much to talk over with her friends.

Was this the first step towards gaining freedom for women? It would certainly be a most difficult one! For a woman to force her way into the jealously-guarded ranks of the medical profession was almost, but not quite, an impossibility, as the struggles of Dr. Elizabeth Blackwell served to prove.

IMPORTANT DECISION

Emily Davies took up the idea with enthusiasm, and when Elizabeth returned home her mind was made up. She was going to be a doctor—the first woman doctor in Britain!

When she broke the news to her parents they were surprised and puzzled. They thought the idea rather disgusting, and, of course, would have preferred their daughter to remain at home in happy idleness, enjoying the usual social round.

But they did not actively oppose her, as Florence Nightingale's parents had done some twenty years earlier.

They were anxious about allowing her to enter such an untried life, but she convinced them that she could not live without some real work.

In the end her father consented and hinted that if she persevered and had any success, she could count on his active help.

So Elizabeth went to work first to fill in the gaps in her education. A local schoolmaster coached her in Greek and Latin. Miss Emily Davies, who wrote beautiful English, offered to correct any essays and papers her young friend cared to send.

When Elizabeth's friends found out what she intended to do, they laughed her to scorn. This put Mr. Garrett on his mettle. He declared that he would *prefer* a woman doctor to attend his wife and daughters if he could be certain that she was thoroughly qualified.

From the painting in the possession of the Royal Free Hospital, London
DR. ELIZABETH BLACKWELL

No one was going to laugh at his Elizabeth! He would help her, and together they would succeed!

So he went with her to call on various doctors in Harley Street, but not one of them offered any encouragement. Not one would take her as student.

At last a Dr. Hawes, who had some influence with the Middlesex Hospital, suggested that she should go into the surgical ward of that hospital for six months.

LOUIS PASTEUR, 1822–1895

He thought this would be a good test of her determination and her staying power, for at that time conditions in the surgical wards were very bad indeed.

Pasteur had just proved that many diseases were caused by germs. But another six or eight years was to go by before Joseph Lister, working in a Glasgow hospital, showed that after a cut or an operation the wound was open to the attack of the numerous germs or bacteria which existed all around.

In 1860 his antiseptic system of surgery had not been perfected. The sterilization of instruments was unknown. Doctors operated without gloves and often with unwashed hands.

So it was not surprising that patients who survived an operation often died of the septic poisoning and gangrene which followed.

Dr. Hawes knew that the sights and sounds and smells in a surgical ward were enough to sicken anyone whose devotion and determination were not of the highest quality.

AT WORK IN THE WARDS

On 1st August, 1860, Elizabeth, equipped with a linen apron and a notebook, entered the Middlesex Hospital. Her quiet, grave manner pleased the matron and nurses who received her kindly. Soon they were teaching her how to dress wounds and how to care for the patients.

The doctors were quite friendly and talked to her freely about their work, but many of their explanations were difficult for her to grasp owing to her lack of elementary training.

Her position in the hospital was rather irregular, and this troubled her. She was not a nurse and the authorities would not take her as a medical student. The hospital would only receive male students.

However, after a while the Medical Board agreed that, though they would not take a fee and so recognize her as a student, they would accept a donation and allow her to stay at the hospital as an amateur, learning all she could as she went round the wards.

They also put at her disposal a room where she could do dissecting away from the male students, for they said the presence of a lady at lectures would distract the men's attention!

But by May, 1861, the doctors with whom she worked spoke so well of her that the heads of the Hospital Board withdrew their opposition and allowed her to attend some of the lectures.

JOSEPH LISTER, 1827–1912

For a time all went well. Then, unfortunately, there came a day when a visiting physician asked the class a question which none of the boys could answer. Elizabeth, rather timidly, gave the right reply.

Immediately there was an angry buzz in the room and the young faces turned in her direction wore ugly scowls. Elizabeth realized that she would have done better to keep silent.

The next day the majority of the students, irate and jealous, sent a petition to the hospital committee demanding the dismissal of the female, and her exclusion from all further lectures.

So poor Elizabeth had to withdraw.

"I feel somewhat adrift," she wrote to Emily Davies, "but not unduly crushed. God will keep us in His service if we try to see what and where it is."

Another friend writing to Elizabeth soon afterwards said:

"No, dear Miss Garrett, we will not, we cannot pity you, because you have a spirit which places you above all circumstances. The manner in which you have acted makes us respect and admire you the more. But we cannot help grieving for the Women's Cause, which must suffer so much if you are baffled."

Elizabeth was determined that the Cause should not suffer. She went on fighting, but always in a courteous and ladylike way, which won the admiration of all.

UNDAUNTED BY SETBACKS

The lecturers themselves regretted the decision to exclude her, saying that "her conduct had been marked by a union of judgment and delicacy which had commanded their entire esteem," but they now had no choice in the matter.

After the success of Miss Blackwell the British Medical Association had declared that no one with only a foreign qualification would be allowed to practice in Britain. And as no college would examine a woman and so allow her to gain a British qualification, the position seemed hopeless.

MIDDLESEX HOSPITAL

"You might as well go to America and get your training there," the head of the Medical Board told Elizabeth.

But Elizabeth was not so easily beaten. She was determined to fight her way into the English schools and so open a door through which other English girls could enter an honoured profession and be sure of a welcome.

So she went on working eight hours a day in the wards, and spent her evenings studying Latin, chemistry and anatomy, with the help of two doctors who agreed to give her some private tuition.

Elizabeth was a very modest girl, and though she could hold to her own opinions in a quiet, determined way, she never prided herself on having greater intellectual gifts than other people.

At times she felt dissatisfied with her progress and her want of power. "It is hard to be satisfied with a gooseberry nature, when one sees that a peach is wanted," she said. "I have always known that my powers were of a kind to make success difficult," she went on. "Perhaps the Cause will not be injured by this. Probably the majority of women are not much more gifted than I am, so my example may be more useful than it would from a more brilliant person."

She thought herself very plain and without charm, but she made the best of herself and did not despise good clothes, like some women who devoted themselves to higher education and the Cause.

Of one of her friends, who agreed to study chemistry with her, she wrote:

"Miss Drewry looks awfully strong-minded in walking dress. She has short petticoats and a close, round hat and several other dreadfully ugly arrangements. It is a serious mistake, I think, for **a** respectable woman to dress like this.

"When my student life begins I shall try to get some self-coloured dresses of a serviceable but rich material, which will do without trimming."

Her portraits show that she was not at all the plain girl she imagined herself to be, and if, as she said, she lacked charm she possessed the great gift of being able to make and keep many friends.

A STEP FORWARD

Elizabeth had been working very hard for many months, so she decided to spend the remainder of the summer with her family at Aldeburgh.

She did not allow disappointment to make her bitter or unhappy, but while at home helped to entertain guests and joined in the picnics, sports and other social affairs arranged by her sisters and their friends.

Towards the end of August she was overjoyed to receive a letter saying that the Society of Apothecaries would be forced by their charter to allow her to sit for their examinations, if she could arrange for the usual lectures and the necessary five years' experience in clinics and hospitals.

Elizabeth was delighted. If she passed these examinations she would be awarded a diploma which would give her the licence to practice as a doctor. It would not be a degree, and Elizabeth was determined to gain her M.D.

But it was a step in the right direction, and back went Elizabeth to London, full of courage and hope.

Her studies could be arranged privately. But since no hospital would take her as a medical student, she had to gain her experience the hard way, by attending various hospitals as a nurse.

Occasionally she came across helpful doctors, but usually they and their students were only anxious to discourage and annoy this young woman who persisted in trying to work her way into the medical world which, they felt, should be kept exclusively for men.

JOINT ENTERPRISE

Though her work kept her very busy, she found time to join a group of friends who had started a bureau, the first of its kind, to help women to find paid work.

With high hopes and burning enthusiasm this little group of women from comfortable homes set themselves to aid their less fortunate sisters, and to free women of ail ranks from the bonds and fetters with which they were shackled.

Elizabeth threw herself into everything with keenness and zest, and as she loved talking to intelligent people who *did* things she enjoyed thoroughly the occasional parties given by her various friends.

While working for her Apothecaries Licence she never forgot that she intended finally to win the Degree of Doctor of Medicine, and since the English Universities would not even allow her to matriculate, she went to Scotland.

Here she had the usual struggle. One doctor to whom she wrote asking for instruction in anatomy replied:

"It is not necessary that fair ladies should be brought into contact with such foul scenes . . . they would make bad doctors."

Another wrote:

"I am among the warmest advocates for the cultivation of the mind of women, but I will never consent to unsex them."

Each letter—and there were many of them—was like a slap in the face to the anxious Elizabeth, but she never lost hope, and by the end of 1865 the worst of the struggle was over.

RESOLUTE CANDIDATE

By 1865, after, nearly six years of constant study under most difficult circumstances, Elizabeth had passed all the necessary preliminary examinations, so she applied to the Society of Apothecaries for permission to sit for her final.

The Board of Examiners tried to refuse, but Mr. Garrett reminded them of their letter of four years ago. His daughter had fulfilled her side of the bargain; they must now fulfil theirs.

So, unwillingly, they allowed Elizabeth to sit for the examination. She passed with credit and so obtained the L.S.A. Diploma.

The members of the society were so annoyed to think that a woman had forced her way into their private province that they immediately altered their regulations. In future, they said, all candidates for their diploma must work through a recognized medical school.

And since medical schools were for men only, this was another door slammed in the face of women.

But Elizabeth Garrett had carved the wedge which very soon was to force this and other doors wide open.

In the following year her name was entered in the Medical Register, and she, the first woman doctor in England, opened the Dispensary for Women and Children in the Marylebone Road district.

She also, with the help of her father, took a house in Upper Berkeley Street, and there started a private practice, which grew rapidly. For, in spite of what all the doctors said to the contrary, there were many women who preferred to be treated by one of their own sex.

*   *   *   *   *

Shortly after her success, Elizabeth suffered the first great sorrow of her life. In 1867 she lost her beloved eldest sister, Louisa Smith.

The two had been almost inseparable, for when in London Elizabeth had spent many months each year in her sister's home.

Louisa left four young children, and Elizabeth felt it both a duty and a great joy to care for these as though they were her own. Two or three times a week, whatever her engagements, she went down to see them and lavished on them the love and care of a mother.

*   *   *   *   *

In 1869 she became an honorary member of the Shadwell Hospital for Children, and was elected to the Board of Management. On this Board she frequently met, among other interesting people, a Mr. J. G. S. Anderson, with whom she became very friendly.

HONOURED IN FRANCE

By this time the University of Paris had thrown open its medical schools to women. Elizabeth was the first woman to take advantage of this.

She was no great linguist, and she knew that answering difficult questions in a foreign language would be no light task.

Also she was very busy with her clinic and her private patients, but she knew that the Paris M.D. would be well worth having, so she set to work with a will.

By getting up very early in the mornings and by studying as she drove to see her patients, she prepared for the French examinations and passed all six of them with credit.

In June, 1870, she became the first woman M.D. of the University of Paris, one of the finest medical schools in the world.

All this time other pioneers were struggling to help women to obtain their freedom.

Miss Emily Davies, who had come to London in 1860, was working hard to force or persuade the Universities to throw open their examinations to women. By 1865 she had gained permission for girls to take the Cambridge Local Examinations, and in the following year she founded the London School Mistresses' Association.

ELIZABETH GARRETT ANDERSON FACES HER EXAMINERS AT THE FACULTY OF MEDICINE IN THE UNIVERSITY OF PARIS

At the same time she was trying to organize Colleges for Women; largely through her influence Girton College was founded in Cambridge.

In 1873 she became its first head mistress, and for many years carefully steered it to success and fame.

In 1867 Elizabeth's young sister, Millicent, married Henry Fawcett, a professor at Cambridge University and M.P. for

Brighton. She and her husband both worked hard for the Higher Education of Women and largely through them Newnham College was founded.

Millicent also became President of the National Union of Women's Suffrage Societies and with many others worked for the day when women would be allowed to vote.

By 1869 they had won for women the right to vote for Municipal Councils, but many years were to pass before women were granted the Parliamentary vote.

Elizabeth did not speak at suffrage meetings, but she gave the movement her wholehearted support.

CONTINENTAL ADVENTURE

In the summer of this same year, 1870, war broke out between Germany and France. Elizabeth's sympathies were entirely with the French, who were suffering many defeats at the hands of the Germans.

In September she had a few days' leisure, so she determined to take her young brother and sister, Sam and Josephine, over to the Continent for a short holiday in Antwerp and Brussels.

Armies did not move as rapidly in those days as they do now, and she had no fear of not being able to get home again.

The little party did, however, get caught up in the march, and at one point "found it quite impossible to get a biscuit or a bed."

A Prussian officer allowed them to ride in one of the ambulance waggons going to Sedan with hospital stores.

When they arrived at that town they could not find beds. Every hotel was full, so they approached another Prussian officer, and he kindly took them to his home, giving up his room to the two women for the night.

The next day, when they turned homewards, they were held up at a small station for three or four hours.

As trainloads of wounded came through and halted there, Josephine distributed chocolate and tobacco to the men while Sam and Elizabeth helped to dress their wounds.

THE DINING HALL AT GIRTON COLLEGE, CAMBRIDGE, IN 1877

Soon after the Garretts reached England the Germans besieged Paris. Among the many foreigners who fled from the doomed city were two American ladies who reached London, friendless and ill.

They consulted the only woman doctor in the city, Elizabeth Garrett, and she, after examining them, feared they had the dreaded disease of smallpox.

No hotel or lodgings would receive them in that condition, and no hospital for infectious diseases existed nearby, so Elizabeth, in the kindness of her heart, put these strangers to bed in her own house, and kept them with her until they were quite recovered.

EDUCATION REFORM

The year 1870 was a very full and busy one for Elizabeth. In that year the Government passed an Act which gave the country, for the first time, a system of Elementary Education.

This meant that each borough had to appoint a school board, or committee to manage the affairs of the schools in its area.

Elizabeth Garrett's patients and their husbands asked her to allow them to propose her as a candidate for the School Board in Marylebone.

She did so, and though at that date women seldom spoke at public meetings, Elizabeth soon found herself addressing audiences both indoors and out.

She soon developed into a clear and ready, often amusing, speaker, and though she had to overcome many prejudices she won much hearty praise.

One of her friends was afraid that her head would be turned by all the publicity and praise, but she wrote in reply:

"I *do* rejoice in every gift, however trifling, that makes me more fit for the special niche I am meant to fill, but I don't think this really hurts me.

"The corrective is found in not living a self-centred life, in caring for great things, and in an enthusiasm of admiration for those before whom oneself is pigmied."

The election took place on 30th November, and when the result was known it was found that Elizabeth topped the poll by a tremendous majority.

This result was a great victory not only for her, but for the whole of the women's movement. She became a well-known and popular figure, and was able to gain more and more support for the Cause.

A HAPPY MARRIAGE

This year, too, was memorable for her in still another sphere. The work for the election, and for the improvement of the Shadwell Hospital, had brought her into frequent contact with Mr. James Anderson, the son of a Scottish Minister and himself a member of an important shipping firm. He was a man with an equal and pleasant temper, and an unfailing fund of wit and humour.

James and Elizabeth had many interests in common, and they grew more and more friendly. Before the end of the year they were deeply in love with each other, and just before Christmas they became engaged.

When Elizabeth's friends heard of the engagement many of them were very uneasy. They feared that marriage would make her give up her work, both as a doctor and as a leader of the women's movement.

But she said firmly: "A man's career does not end with marriage, so why should a woman's? Love must not make us selfish, and I will not choose my own happiness at the price of the duty I owe to women, who need something which I, as one of the leaders, can give.

"I am sure the woman question will never be solved so long as marriage is thought to interfere with freedom and an independent career.

"I think there is a good chance that my marriage may do something to discourage this idea."

She decided that she would not give up the name by which she was now well known. She would be called Elizabeth Garrett Anderson. She had no intention of giving up her career as a doctor, or of meanly deserting her post as a Leader in the Women's Cause.

*   *   *   *   *

Neither of them ever forgot that Christmas Eve when Elizabeth first introduced James to the family.

Mr. and Mrs. Garrett were inclined to be gloomy, and the two young daughters, Agnes and Josephine, were very critical. Elizabeth was thirty-four! Fancy thinking of marriage at her age! Ridiculous! And what would the man be like?

The family was waiting in the holly-decked hall when the brougham, drawn by the old mare, drew up. The door opened and the soft light of the oil-lamp fell on a radiant Elizabeth and a tall, pleasant-looking man whose courtesy soon won the hearts of the old people.

Before many days had passed he had captivated the young

ones, too. He was friendly and amusing, and he was a great one at charades.

He spoke with a slight Socttish accent, could dance the Highland fling, sing a good song and skate skilfully over the frozen marshes.

He never talked to them on "dry" subjects such as the higher education of women, but, when other entertainment failed, told them amusing stories.

The holiday in Aldeburgh was a very brief one. Soon Elizabeth and James were back in the capital and Elizabeth was writing in her witty manner: "I should very much like to be married in London, entirely without millinery and almost without cookery!"

EMILY DAVIES

The wedding took place six weeks later at the Presbyterian Church, Marylebone. The service was a simple one, "without millinery," but not entirely "without cookery." Several of the guests travelled some distance to be present, and even a journey across London in a growler or a hansom, with delays at the toll gate on the bridge, meant an early start. So a wedding breakfast was provided.

HAPPINESS AND SUCCESS

Elizabeth now entered on a period of great happiness. She and her husband loved each other dearly. Theirs was a perfect partnership, and James' companionship helped to mellow and to soften her.

Her struggles had tended to harden her, her successes had made her just a little bit proud. She was in danger of becoming "the stern pioneer."

Now, though James gloried in her success and took a great interest in all her work, he teased her and laughed at her kindly if she gave herself airs. She took his raillery in good part. The growing arrogance disappeared and she became once more the humble, kindly, loving Elizabeth of her younger days.

Her life was a very full and busy one, and when her first baby, Louisa, was born in 1873 she felt that she could no longer give the necessary time to the London School Board.

So she did not stand for re-election, and her place was taken by her young sister Alice, now Mrs. Herbert Cowell.

Another baby girl, Margaret, was born the following year, and six months later, as a very capable and devoted nurse, "Aaa" was in charge of the children, Elizabeth and her sister Millicent went off for a short visit to Rome.

They enjoyed themselves thoroughly and became quite young again, as, among other things, they made tea in a hotel bedroom and drank it from a tumbler! "It's a great economy and such fun," wrote the eternal schoolgirl, Elizabeth.

She wrote to and received letters from James every day, and wished constantly that he was with her.

When they reached Rome the two English women were presented to the great Italian patriot and liberator, Garibaldi, for whom they had a tremendous admiration and respect.

To the great grief of her parents little Margaret died in December, 1875.

Two years later a baby boy was born and christened Alan.

Elizabeth's days were very full with her husband, her children, her patients, and some lectures she was giving to women students.

But she found time to enjoy life to the full. Hard work was enlivened by occasional trips abroad and parties at home.

"I do like meeting my fellow creatures," she wrote. "I begin to think it is one mark of a good heart to like to go to evening parties!"

But however engrossed she was in her own life, she followed with interest the careers of other women who were trying to broaden the trail which she had first blazed through the thicket of prejudice, jealousy and ignorance.

STUDENT INSURGENTS

One such group of girls, led by Sophia Jex-Blake, had applied to the University of Edinburgh for medical training.

To their great delight, though their lectures and demonstrations had to be taken apart from the boys, they were allowed to matriculate, so they settled down to some years of hard work, and did extremely well in their examinations.

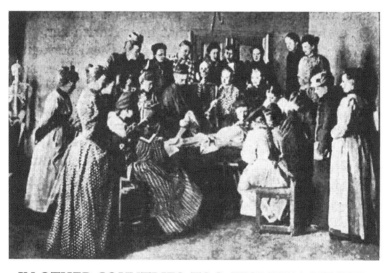

IN OTHER COUNTRIES, TOO, WOMEN AGITATED
TO ENTER PROFESSIONS HITHERTO EXCLUSIVE
TO MEN. HERE A DOCTOR IS GIVING LESSONS IN
ANATOMY TO SWEDISH WOMEN IN 1880

One of the group actually won a coveted honour, a scholarship in chemistry, but the professor said he could not award the scholarship to a woman. He gave it to the man below her on the examination list!

Imagine the storm this caused! The young women naturally raised the cry of "Injustice," and they had a few male sympathizers.

But many of the male students were bitterly opposed to the little group of women, and at the so-called Riot of Surgeons' Hall actually threw mud at them, and tried to shut them out of the lecture hall.

After this most of the professors of the Medical Schools refused to teach them or even allow them to finish the course. They declared that the University had exceeded its powers when it permitted the girls to matriculate!

The young women, unbeaten, determined to continue the struggle elsewhere. Some of them went to Zurich and Paris. One of them, Sophia Jex-Blake, determined to make a fresh effort in London.

She proposed at once to found a separate Medical School for women.

Elizabeth, though she did not like Sophia's impetuous way of rushing ahead, joined the council of the new school, so as not to cause any split in the ranks of the women pioneers, and the London School of Medicine for Women was opened in 1874.

But the struggle was by no means over. Many well-qualified doctors agreed to give lectures and instruction at the school, but the examining bodies still refused to admit the women to the qualifying examinations and the hospitals refused to allow them in the clinics.

At last the women decided to appeal to Parliament. A deputation, including Elizabeth Garrett Anderson, waited on a Cabinet Minister and asked for Government intervention.

So a Bill was introduced into Parliament and in August, 1876, a new Medical Act was passed.

This gave all British medical examination boards the right to admit women to their qualifying examinations.

Here was success indeed! The fortress which the women had attacked so boldly was shaken! It would not be long now, they thought, before absolute victory was theirs.

In March, 1877, the Royal Free Hospital opened its wards to women students, and in the next year the University of London declared that all its degrees should be available to women on the same terms as to men.

Five years later, 1883, Dr. Elizabeth Garrett Anderson was presented at Court.

The same year she became Dean of the School of Medicine

for Women, and for the rest of her life took an active interest in its development.

Under her guidance and inspiration it made steady progress. During its early years its buildings were very poor and inadequate, and the young women students worked under great difficulties. But they were remarkably successful. Most of them passed their examinations with flying colours, winning gold medals, exhibitions and honours.

Elizabeth was at this time full of energy and courage, vigorous in mind and body. She had a good business head and was never afraid of acting on her own responsibility.

She could express her ideas clearly and forcibly. She could guide and control her committees and usually persude them to her way of thinking.

She was dignified, yet always friendly and approachable, and she had a good and strong influence on the hundreds of students who worked under her.

WIDESPREAD INTERESTS

The School of Medicine was by no means Elizabeth's only interest.

You will remember that as soon as she was recognized as a doctor in 1866 she not only began a private practice from her house in Upper Berkeley Street, but also opened St. Mary's Dispensary for Women in Seymour Place, a crowded district near Marylebone Road.

Here she attended out-patients three times a week, and often visited women of the neighbourhood in their own homes.

For several years she was the only doctor to visit this Dispensary, which filled a crying need and which soon became very popular.

Numerous patients crowded the little waiting-room. By 1871 nine thousand names were on the books, and forty thousand visits had been paid.

Some patients came in from the country, so anxious were they to be treated by a woman. A few of these were so ill that they were unable to face the return journey, so beds had to be provided for them.

By 1872 there were ten beds and the Dispensary was renamed the New Hospital for Women.

Still the demand grew, and with the help of a few generous friends three more houses were bought in Marylebone Road and the new hospital transferred there.

The number of patients continued to increase so rapidly that in 1887 a public appeal was made, for the first time, to provide a building fund.

Elizabeth and her helpers worked tremendously hard, organizing appeals, bazaars and social meetings, and by the end of the year they reached their target of £20,000. The new building in the Euston Road provided forty-two beds and an ophthalmic department.

As the number of women doctors increased, more and more of them gave their services to the hospital, but for nearly twenty years Elizabeth was the only one who would undertake difficult surgical cases.

THE NEW HOSPITAL FOR WOMEN, WHICH WAS LATER RE-NAMED THE ELIZABETH GARRETT ANDERSON HOSPITAL

She was extremely anxious before these serious operations, and never enjoyed this part of her work. Though she was very successful she was glad when, in later years, skilled women surgeons were able to relieve her.

In 1892, when the Hospital for Women was firmly established, Elizabeth resigned and left the work in younger hands.

When accepting her resignation the committee paid her a great tribute.

One member said: "The hospital owes not only its foundation, but its great and continuous success to Mrs. Garrett Anderson's indomitable energy and ability. The recognition and established position now enjoyed by medical women in England is due to her perseverance and enthusiasm for the Cause."

ELIZABETH'S CHILDREN

In spite of all her work and her many interests, Elizabeth kept up a large correspondence. She wrote frequently to her friends, at least once a week to her parents, and usually twice a week to her children when they were away at school.

Louie was at St. Leonard's School, and Alan at Eton. In May, 1891, he wrote the following about a photograph of himself and his dog, a large black-and-tan collie, seated together on a sofa:

"I wish Don was separated from me, because I don't like always looking at myself and I do like looking at Don."

Later he wrote: "I have gummed up Don in my room!"

Elizabeth wrote always with goose quills, the pens of her youth. She cut them herself and never liked anyone to touch them.

She never had a steel pen, a fountain-pen or a typewriter. Nor would she have a secretary. Day after day she ploughed through a mass of correspondence which would have overwhelmed most people, and answered most of the letters in her own strong, clear handwriting.

She made many friends and liked having visitors in her

home. She was fond of young people and her nieces and nephews often stayed with her. As she was always busy, she expected them to amuse themselves during the day.

"There, my dears!" she would say at breakfast, giving them each a golden sovereign. "Go and amuse yourselves until evening. But remember, dinner is at seven—prompt!"

After dinner she would devote herself to them, arranging parties or taking them to the theatre.

"You know, my dears," she often said to them, "people can be divided into two sorts—the *givers* and the *getters*. You, I hope, are going to be found in the first class."

At other times she would express some impatience with miserable, grumpy people: "There is no point in spreading gloom around you," she would say. "Be one of the *radiants*, my dear, not one of the *absorbents*."

To the general public she appeared a capable, practical person who had fought a good fight, not only for herself, but for all womankind. The fight had made her perhaps a little brusque in manner. But those nearest to her knew that her heart was very tender.

FURTHER BITTERNESS AROUSED

In 1873, eight years after she had qualified as a doctor, Elizabeth had became a member of the Paddington branch of the British Medical Association.

This association was a kind of Union and Club. It protected the rights and interests of medical men and guided young doctors as to their correct behaviour and the courtesies expected from them.

At branch meetings members met and discussed professional difficulties and experiences.

Elizabeth felt that women doctors must claim their right to belong to this Association. To be excluded from it would be regarded as a slight.

ELIZABETH GARRETT ANDERSON ADDRESSES A WOMEN'S SUFFRAGE MEETING IN 1884

She herself was accepted without question by the Paddington Branch, but when, two years later, she attended a General Meeting in Edinburgh, a terrific storm burst over her head.

The President of that period was bitterly opposed to women doctors, and for several days Elizabeth was not allowed to read the paper which she had prepared. When, however, she was given permission to do so it was very well received.

The following year, when the Association met at Bath, it proposed to add to its rules a clause which said that "no female should be eligible as a member of the Association."

Elizabeth made a speech which charmed the meeting, but the motion was passed.

Her appointment was legal and she could not be expelled, but for nineteen years she remained the only woman member of the B.M.A.

What courage it took to attend their meetings and join in their discussions through all those years! But she persisted in doing so.

"Sometimes the feeling of disapproval becomes almost unbearable," she wrote. But she would not let down the Cause by staying away.

Gradually her perseverance, pleasant manners and quiet common sense thawed the ice, and in 1892 the clause excluding women was repealed.

Another victory for Elizabeth and for the women for whom she worked!

By this time there were one hundred and thirty-five medical women registered in England, and by an overwhelming majority they were now allowed to become members of that exclusive body, the B.M.A.

Their acceptance was complete!

*　　　*　　　*　　　*　　　*

By 1897 the School of Medicine for Women, even with the additions which had been made in the past fourteen years, was much too small for the number of students requesting admission.

So, with Elizabeth's help and encouragement, efforts were made to raise a large sum of money to build an entirely new block of buildings.

This was done, and in 1901 the School was recognized as one of the Colleges of the University of London.

ACTIVE RETIREMENT

In 1903 at the age of sixty-seven, Elizabeth Garrett Anderson retired from her position as Dean of the School.

She became, however, its President and thus, though she had resigned her duties to younger hands, she was still able to take an active interest in the work of the students and the progress of the school.

She and her husband retired to Aldeburgh, and though the journey to London was still a trying one for an old lady, she seldom missed any committee meetings or social functions.

In 1913 she encouraged and supported a further building scheme, and promised to give £1,000 a year for three years towards the new extension. This was opened in 1916 by her late Majesty Queen Mary.

In spite of all her work and her many struggles, Elizabeth was, all through her life, a woman of many interests.

She was fond of reading and of doing fine embroidery. Though she played the piano, she was no great musician, but she arranged for Aldeburgh to have concerts of classical music by good artists, and she introduced home industries into the little town.

She was also a keen gardener. "Mrs. Anderson be a power of help to me," said the hired man.

After her retirement she busied herself in the garden every day until her strength began to fail.

In his later years James, her husband, spent much of his time at the golf club which he had started in Aldeburgh a quarter of a century earlier. This had been the means of attracting many visitors to the place. So the little decaying fishing village began to grow prosperous and gradually it developed into the popular seaside resort it is to-day.

James was also elected Mayor of the town he had served so well, and when, to Elizabeth's grief, he died in 1907, she was invited to take up his office for the rest of the year.

The following year she agreed to stand for election. She was chosen almost unanimously and thus became the first woman to hold the office of Mayor.

Late one night, during her period of office, news reached her of the death of King Edward VII. It was too late to do anything that night, but early next morning she was heard pounding on the door of the Deputy Mayor, Mr. Hall.

"Good gracious, Mrs. Anderson!" said that gentleman, looking out from his bedroom window, "you are very early!"

"Not too early!" cried the vigorous old lady. "Don't you know the King is dead, and arrangements must be made for the Proclamation?"

A few hours later, from the steps of the old Moot Hall, she lead the Proclamation announcing the accession of George V to the Throne.

On public occasions such as this, though she was now an old lady of seventy-four, she did her best to maintain the dignity of her office.

Wearing her mayoral robe and chain, her stout, laced boots, her black velvet bonnet, and carrying a rolled-up umbrella in her hand, she stepped out bravely at the head of the procession, preceded only by the macebearer.

Behind her walked the members of the Corporation in their robes; the Lifeboat crew, in which her father had played an heroic part; the local company of Volunteers, and, last of all, the Boy Scouts.

It seemed to many an onlooker very fitting that this woman who had fought so hard to win freedom, independence and equality for the women of her land, should, now, in her declining years, have the honour of leading such a procession.

SUFFRAGETTES AT WESTMINSTER, 1910. THE CELEBRATED MRS. PANKHURST (*right*) WITH DR. GARRETT ANDERSON

PIONEER MEDICAL UNIT

In 1914, when the first World War broke out, Elizabeth's powers were failing, but she insisted on going to London to see her daughter, Dr. Louisa Garrett Anderson, and Dr. Flora Murray leave for France in charge of the first unit of medical women to go abroad.

They were well equipped with drugs, chloroform and surgical instruments which she had helped to provide. That they were able to go at all, this well-trained body of devoted women, was largely due to this old lady of seventy-eight, who, as a young girl, had put up such a valiant struggle.

"My dears," she said to the doctors, "if you succeed in this task you will put forward the Women's Cause by thirty years."

And how right she was! When the war was over, the Government felt that they could no longer deny the vote, and with it the full recognition of independence, to the women who had stood shoulder to shoulder with men in many of the most difficult and dangerous jobs of the war years.

Elizabeth did not live to see this success, but her younger sister, Millicent Fawcett, who for many years had been the leader of the Suffragists, lived until 1929, and so had the satisfaction of seeing women not only able to vote, but also able to sit in Parliament on equal terms with men.

She herself was created a Dame of the British Empire, and her name is enshrined in stone in Westminster Abbey, among the nation's great.

For their services in the medical field Elizabeth's son, Alan, was knighted and awarded the K.B.E. while her daughter, Louisa, was awarded the C.B.E.

How Elizabeth would have rejoiced in her children's honour! But her life came to a peaceful close in December, 1917, and she was buried in the churchyard of her beloved Aldeburgh.

THE ELIZABETH GARRETT ANDERSON HOSPITAL, EUSTON ROAD, LONDON, AS IT IS TO-DAY

Elizabeth had carried happiness in her heart and had radiated happiness around her. She had helped to bring great comfort and joy to hundreds of women of her own generation and to many thousands then unborn.

Her finest memorial is the hospital which, after her death, was re-named the Elizabeth Garrett Anderson Hospital. Her name is enshrined in the hearts of women of all ages who love their independence and who honour the pioneers who helped to win that independence for them.

Printed in Great Britain
by Amazon